Also by Adrianna P. Wilder

A Prayerful Disturbance

21
DAYS
WITH
HIM
For the Single Lady

Adrianna P. Wilder, MPH

21 Days with Him

For the Single Lady

DEDICATION

To all the single women who are seeking wholeness and intimacy with God, while waiting for your mate, this is for you.

To the initial members of my amazing *Whole Single Woman* admin and support team: Tiffany Cole, Shenicka Jones, and Latesha Newsome. You have helped me keep going through joy, pain, sickness and loss. I love you and my prayer is that every seed you have sown into *Whole Single Woman* would be returned back to you in time, money, prayer and love. Praying for your mates!!!

To my first *Whole Single Woman* online cohort in 2021. You were the culmination of years of prayer and contending for women who, at that time, were like me--single. You said "yes" to 11 weeks of rigorous inner-healing and prayer. May you bear much fruit.

Finally, to the future cohorts and members of *Whole Single Woman*, prayer is the purest form of intimacy and will get you closer to destiny than any effort of your human strength. I encourage you to pray, contend and simply wait on God.

FOREWORD

The first time I met Adrianna, I was in a season of deep heartache and pain. My marriage was on the rocks, the new role of mother was heavy, and I felt so alone. My track record with friendships could have been better, so I was not in a space to honestly accept or offer an invitation from anyone.

Adrianna had no idea what I needed, nor did I. But God knew what we both needed 5+ years ago. He knew we needed each other and made sure our paths collided when they did.

Becoming friends with Adrianna radically changed my life in all the best ways; getting a front seat and an invitation to her life one-on-one has been one of the greatest honors of my life.

I met my sweet friend, like a dollar bill, when she was single! I can remember all the times we spoke on the phone about her relationship status and her dreams of her future marriage. We cried, laughed, prayed, and waited for the physical manifestation of her Husband.

In her season of singleness, my friend was committed to Christ, her call, her community, her family, and her friendships. Her desire to please the Lord in all she did never wavered, even when times got rough. I remember watching her in awe. Her walk and commitment to her purpose inspired me in more ways than one.

So you better believe when she met her now husband Kenneth, I was rejoicing in wonder at the beautiful work God had done.

Adrianna did not choose to stop sharing the promises of God after getting married. She decided to share her story of hope and faith with women still walking and waiting for the promise of their future Husbands to come to fruition.

The model of ministry, encouragement, and strategy the Lord has given her for this time is timely and needed. My Husband and I have served singles through The One University for over 8+ years. We have seen the ebb and flow of what singles are hungering and needing today.

I am proud to confidently say that my friend and sister is sound, tested, and anointed to speak hope and life into the lives of singles worldwide. Her devotional, *21 Days with Him for the Single Lady*, is a manual and blueprint to help every single woman find peace, contentment, hope, and purpose in their season of waiting for their husbands.

If you are tired on the journey and must be reminded that God is for you and your future marriage, this devotional is for you! May you take the words of this devotional and apply them to your life and see his will for covenant come forth in a way that only He can do.

Natasha Ann Miller
The Praying Mama, Founder
The One University, Co-Founder

21

DAYS
WITH
HIM

For the Single Lady

INTRODUCTION

I remember when my journey with God started. Well, I remember when I said "yes" to the drawing of Holy Spirit. The beginning happened long before that, but my "yes" was the beginning of my rebirth. I was 16 years old. I had been running from God for two years. I was tired of church and the mundane Christian walk—I wanted more. As a result, He gave me more. He gave me encounter.

Personally, I had picked a much different life than what He designed and navigated me through. I thought I would be married early, on a foreign mission field or serving on church staff. And though I did the latter two, marriage was not in the stars for me early on. Oh, how I wanted it to be. I wanted to marry my high school sweetheart, have kids and travel the world while raising them and serve the Lord next to him. But God's divine and perfect nature had something much better for me. Now looking back on my journey, I am so glad I did not get what I thought I wanted…I got something so much better.

In my 22-year walk with God, I came to know Him so intimately. My gifts and talents were developed; my sensitivity to

His voice was refined; and my ability to move with His promptings was honed. I can honestly say that "I know God." As the old saints said, "You can't make me doubt Him. I know too much about Him." This is how I feel.

I have walked through some significant trauma and testing. You would not believe the half of it if I told you, but I will never speak of much of it until eternity, but it remains true that there is a story to tell. However, without Christ, I would not have made it through. He has been my Confidant, my Friend and my Savior. In fact, it has been through the highs and lows of my life that I understood Him. Yes, some of the lows were a result of my zeal, sin and pride, but at the end of it all, I still found Him there with arms wide open helping me pick up the pieces.

When I sing, preach or testify, I close my eyes and I see Him. The One who has seen me through again and again. When I talk of Him, He is not a distant friend, but a close dance partner that remains with me even when I don't want it or can't see it. He is real. This book is a book to encourage the single lady. Women reach out to me all the time who want to learn from my relationship with God, who have questions about my love for Jesus or who simply want to know how and why I am so passionate about Him. This book is designed to spark intimacy, passion and practical prayer.

Prayer.

Prayer is the basis for everything. The dialogue with God is what has seen me through. Dialogue is intimacy and the more I talk with Him, the more intimate we become. Likewise, the more you talk with Him, the more intimate you will become with Him. I don't care if I am teaching a class, a seminar, leading worship

or simply doing one-on-one mentoring—you better believe I am
going to talk about intimacy with God. A life void of intimacy is a
life void of prayer. And, a life void of prayer is a life void of purpose.
You must pray.

In the following pages you will see that the first fourteen days of
this journey is about you and God. Each day is a snippet taken from
my own life and then a prayer to accompany the topical discussion.
I encourage you to read the prayer out loud, make notes in the
book and journal heavily as God breathes revelation into your soul.
The last seven days of this journey allows you to take your pen
and write prayers for your future mate. As you grow in prayer for
yourself, God will reveal His true heart to you. As He reveals it, you
will know how to pray for your future mate. Your desires that may
be selfish in nature, will slip away and what remains will be His
heart for your future spouse. I believe if you desire marriage, God
desires to fulfill it. He is not a God that teases us, but wants us to
live life in full, right here where we are. Marriage is a part of that
fullness if you desire it. This book will help you go deep with Him,
so He can reveal His heart to you.

I prayed for my mate long before he was on the scene. Mind
you, a lot of my prayers were cries where I was mad at God,
begging for my mate and yelling at the seemingly unjust nature of
Him making me wait; nonetheless, they were prayers. I am a firm
believer in the Formational Flow of Prayer (FFP)[1] —especially
when it comes to desires. The Formational Flow of Prayer is a
concept I came up with to help new believers and people new to

---

[1] Formational Flow of Prayer. Adrianna Wilder. Formational Flow of Prayer Seminar:
Lord Teach Me to Pray. 2023.

prayer understand the beauty that comes from prayer that is not structured. I have been in church a long time and the challenge for people to pray because they think they are doing it wrong has long since been a problem. Prayer is prayer. As you grow in prayer you will mature in prayer, but it is important for Christians to understand that, a prayer that begins is often not a prayer that is perfected. And, that is okay!

Below is an rough example of the FFP in "real time" from my personal walk with God:

> I AM TIRED OF BEING SINGLE. → WHERE ARE YOU GOD? → DO YOU HEAR ME? → YOU DON'T HEAR ME! → I KNOW YOU HEAR ME! → PLEASE HEAR ME NOW! → I KNOW THAT YOU DO. → PLEASE LOOK ON YOUR SERVANT. → REMEMBER YOUR WORD AND PROMISE. → PLEASE ANSWER. → MANIFEST YOUR WORD TO YOUR SERVANT. → EVEN NOW DO IT. → YOU DESIRE THIS FOR ME. → I REMEMBER YOUR WORD. → YOUR PROMISES ARE "YES" AND "AMEN." → I DECREE THAT MY ANSWER IS COMING! → I DECLARE THAT EVEN NOW IT IS HERE. → REMEMBER ME AS I PARTNER WITH YOU. → THIS IS YOUR WILL. → I DECLARE IT IS SO! → IN JESUS' NAME, → I WAIT ON YOU...I KNOW YOU WILL ANSWER...AMEN!

Did you see the progression? It is one of the most beautiful parts of prayer. You see it all throughout the Psalms and if I am honest, my prayers are often still like this–especially in dry seasons. This FFP allows us to pour out our hearts before Him in truth–without shame. This "pour" ultimately makes space for faith which reminds us of the Word. Finally, the reminder of the word causes us to partner with His will and then live from a place of authority by declaring His truth in and for a situation. Prayer allows us to go from defeat to victory and from sadness to tenacious joy!

This book is a book about victory. It is your faith seed into your future. It is your partnership with heaven. So, get ready for a journey that will lead to a voyage with our Savior. Let Him teach you how to pray. Let Him ignite your heart in healing. Let Him guide your hand and heart to sketch a heavenly prayer journal for your future mate. Most importantly, watch your prayers and your dreams come true: "for with God, nothing shall be impossible."[2]

Hey Single Lady, get ready for the journey of a lifetime. Get ready for God!

---

[2] Luke 1:37 (NASB)

DAY 1
THE WILL OF GOD

Ephesians 3:18, 19: "...may be able to comprehend with all the saints what is the width and length and height and depth, and to know the love of Christ which surpasses knowledge, that you may be filled to all the fullness of God."

Before I married, God brought multiple experiences across my path so that I would know how to operate in different realms of influence. If you look at my resume, you will see that I did not box myself in, but I wanted as many varied experiences as possible. I wanted to be full and complete. Now, I didn't see every experience coming, and not every experience was God's best, but I had a simple prayer that I would pray: The will of God: nothing more, nothing less and nothing else. This simple prayer has guided my journey that has led me into the depths of His love time and time again. Everything in the world begins and ends with love. And so, as I prayed for His will, I experienced more love. And the more love I experienced, the more my circumstances, experiences and influence grew and it made me well-rounded. Single woman, you do not have to come from the "right" family, the "right" side of town or even the "right" educational background. You only need Jesus and a prayer and, if you have that, you have all you need in the world. Above all things, pray that you will experience His love and Be full in Him. My God, His love truly DOES satisfy.

Prayer

Dear Lord,

Make us full and complete in You today. Help us to hear and see and know Your magnificent love for us and Your passionate desire for us and our well-being. May You grant us the grace to go deep and the wisdom to live fully in You and Your love. Forgive our pretension and our apprehensions in knowing who You are and who You have called us to be. Help us to hear the truth. According to Your Word which is rich and abundant, we pray that every day we would be strengthened and encouraged with power through the Holy Spirit from the inside out. That in our decision-making process and relationship-making process Christ would be preeminent and that we would trust His process by faith. Let our faith stand on Your love and let this love root us and ground us in seeing things as You see them. May this love give us true vision and blot out all things that come to skew what You truly have for us. Anything that would block our hearing, seeing and knowing Your will, remove it. Let there be a deep comprehension of truth. That where the enemy and our flesh would want to lead us down a wrong path, You guard and protect us so that nothing hinders us from experiencing the true fullness of Christ which is all encompassing in the length, width, depth and height. God, as single women, help us to be full. Help us to not lack. In this time of waiting, let it not be just the matrimonial aspect we so earnestly seek You for, but let it be all the other aspects of our lives. You have full and complete wisdom for every area, so God, as we wait, strengthen our physical bodies, strengthen our financial capacities, strengthen our relationships with others and strengthen our love for ourselves. Let us be full. Let us be complete. Let us be lacking no good thing. God, we don't want to be haphazard in our living. We don't want to just think we are to wait around for a man to do everything, but we want to be sure to pray and seek You to prepare in every way. We want our prayer lives to be full, our spiritual awareness to be keen and our words to be anointed. We don't want to wait unwell. Help us dear Lord, to wait well. Make us full and complete. Take us into the depths of love right now!

In Jesus' Name, Amen!

DAY 2
THE WISDOM WOMAN

◄────────────►

Proverbs 4:7: "Wisdom is the principal thing; therefore get wisdom: and with all thy getting get understanding."

Wisdom is a key principle of everyday living. But how many of us walk around without it or falling short of its full capabilities in our lives? Knowledge without wisdom is dangerous. And this type of danger can prolong receiving an answer to prayer. There is an entire book in the Bible dedicated to wisdom. It teaches us how to walk, talk and move. Its principles are everlasting and come from eternity Himself. Wisdom is vital and necessary. One thing I had to learn, and I am still learning, was how to walk in wisdom. I learned this is sometimes walking down the hard road, but other times, I gleaned it and listened straight from the Bible or from others who have gone before me. How I wish I did that more—the rough road was ugly. Prior to marriage, I studied some verses about a wife and

---

[3] Proverbs 31, 1 Corinthians 7 (NASB)

meditated on them.[3] Once married, I would see them rise out of me and I would have opportunities to walk in wisdom or foolishness. But, because I had digested the Word, the pull to do the wise thing was greater than to do the foolish thing. It is my admonishment that you learn the principles of the Proverbs-type of woman now.

Pray these principles over yourself and then ask God to make them a reality in your life. Additionally, ask for the wisdom needed to live this life and the revelation needed to know Him. So many of us are crying out for purpose and in Ephesians it clearly tells us that He will give wisdom and revelation and that it can only be found in Him. I charge you to get to know Wisdom and get to know Him. Wisdom is Him and this is where your destiny will be found.

Prayer

Dear Lord,

It is so easy to see with our own eyes and hear with our own ears. It is so very easy to not fully interpret what You are saying to our hearts and our minds, but today we want that to stop. Our desire for marriage sometimes supersedes our clarity in prayer and so we do not always pray according to Your will and we sometimes pray amiss. Lord, we choose to make the first thing first. More than knowing who our mate is and more than wanting to know how to attract a man, we seek the wisdom from above. The wisdom on how to be a godly woman and consequently a godly wife. You know it is our desire to hear You, but sometimes in a world so

loud we cannot even hear ourselves and so today we
are choosing to realign our hearts and minds with Your
will to be a woman of wisdom. Firstly, we repent and
ask You for forgiveness, for not aligning our hearts with
wisdom, understanding and instruction. We repent
for doing things out of zeal and angst and not out of
wisdom and your will. Now, Father, we demolish all vain
imaginations not birthed out of the place of wisdom.
May they be demolished and torn down and may they
crumble now. We don't want good ideas, we want God
ideas. And, we don't want just activity, but God activity
that comes from a heart of wisdom. Come Holy Spirit
and today we ask that according to Your word that our
Father, the Father of glory would give to us the spirit of
wisdom and revelation in the knowledge of Jesus. We
know that we are not called by happenstance, but rather
by divine providence and so, Lord, we ask that the vast
richness of Your glory in us and on us be made manifest
and clear. We declare that even now the Holy Spirit is
working within us with strength, power and wisdom.
Even now there is a veil lifted and a strength gifted. Even
now there is a power manifested to see, to handle and
to taste the truth of God's Word and the truth of our
destinies in Him. We will not be thwarted, rerouted or
bamboozled out of our destinies any longer. Wisdom is
our portion. We consciously choose to see His will and
not our own, we will walk into destiny being full and
complete. We choose to see His will. Finally, Abba, each

and every day, please grant us wisdom to know how to move and act in each circumstance so that we not only avoid the traps of the enemy, but we fully walk into the pleasures You have for us without reservation because Your plans are good.

We ask these things in Jesus' name, Amen!

DAY 3
THE CORRECT POSTURE

Luke 7:37b-38: "She brought an alabaster vial of perfume, and standing behind Him at His feet, weeping, she began to wet His feet with her tears, and she wiped them with the hair of her head, and began kissing His feet and anointing them with the perfume."

The funny thing about posture is that it can always be corrected. My first online event with single ladies was called "The Single Lady Chiropractic Adjustment." The goal of that event was to help align and realign some misconceptions and some pitfalls that single ladies fall into while waiting for their mate. These misconceptions and pitfalls have a way of distorting our posture and make us lose our way. It causes aches and pains in our lives that would not otherwise be there if we just chose to wait on God. When I say wait, I don't just mean timing. I also mean waiting on Him and in His presence. When we wait this way, our posture takes on a position that He needs it to have: at His feet. Now in the physical this posture would be bad if one stayed in for a long time, but in the spirit, this posture is the exact place your heart needs to be. Bishop Joseph Garlington says, *"In order to put your heart above your head you must kneel."* And that is how he lives his life. There is a very famous woman from the Bible that also lived this way, Mary Magdalene.[4] She chose to kneel and wash the feet of Jesus. She lowered herself in an act of humility. She submitted herself to Him. This is what kneeling does. This is what the correct posture does. David prayed this simple prayer, "Create in me a clean heart and renew a right spirit in me."[5] As single women, we are to give ourselves wholly to God. It is easy to get out of alignment, but this simple focus, to keep a pure heart and to be righteous and to keep our heart above our heads, will help to stabilize our gaze and center our attention on the One Thing: Jesus.[6] When it comes to marriage, many single women posture themselves with the idea that marriage will solve everything or that the man is meant to be the savior or the one who rescues women from their life of work and the mundane, but this is incorrect. Marriage is not a salvation though it can be a tool of salvation and a husband is not a savior though he can be used to heal and deliver. Before I got married, I realized that I just needed to keep my perception, heart and mind focused on the right things and this would constantly adjust my posture. I fell in love with kneeling.

This day, find yourself in a place of kneeling and even verbally giving yourself over to the One who is Higher in all wisdom and knowledge than you. The One who is worthy of all creation

---

[4] Luke 7:36-39 (NASB)
[5] Psalm 51:10-19 (NASB)
[6] Luke 10:42 (NASB)

kneeling to Him. Let Him daily create in you a clean heart and worship Him with that heart and let Him lead you into truth as you prepare for the Promise.

Prayer

Dear Lord,

I pray today that You will give me the ability to have the correct posture before You. That my heart, mind, will and emotions would be in a posture of humility and a posture to receive all that You have for me. Lord, I have walked in pride and arrogance and in ignorance and I no longer want to walk that way. I want to walk in a way that is pleasing to you, always receiving from You. I want to know when to be busy and when to be still sitting at Your feet. Lord, help me to cultivate a true and beautiful relationship with You. Let me not think that it will start when I get married or when I find a mate, but help me to go deep in intimacy right where I am with You today. Help me to see You as the object of all my affections so that my heart bends and yields to You and You alone. As Mary, knelt at the feet of Jesus, let me lay my life, care and heart at Your feet and from that place listen to Your words of life. I want the correct posture and the good posture that will partner for the plans You have for my life. Remove anxiety and anxious thoughts from me. Remove my desire to make things happen without

You or Your blessing and grant me peace in this waiting process. I know that if I wait and not move in anxiety for fear of missing out, that You will give to me Your very best and my singleness will be worth it. Finally, create in me a clean heart and renew a righteous perception and spirit within me. Jesus, make me whole.

In Jesus' Name, Amen!

DAY 4
PROCESS

John 11:3-6: "So the sisters sent word to Him, saying, 'Lord, behold, he whom You love is sick.' But when Jesus heard this, He said, 'This sickness is not meant for death, but is for the glory of God, so that the Son of God may be glorified by it.' (Now Jesus loved Martha and her sister, and Lazarus.) So when He heard that he was sick, He then stayed two days longer in the place where He was."

God works within systems and processes. He does not work outside of order and what can feel like ordered chaos. Throughout His word, we see God moving and building structure, systems and what we would call institutions to help humans function and live a life with standards and morals and faith. As much as we would like, God will not work outside of process and systems. Just think of the Great Flood with Noah.[7] He gave a strategic blueprint to build an ark and then gave a strategy on what to fill the ark with. Not

---

[7] Genesis 6:9-9:17 (NASB)

only that, He gave the earth approximately 100 years of preaching (process) for them to repent of their sins.[8] He allowed the earth to go through such a process of iniquity that the end result was the flood.

However, in the midst of this process God created a system to save humankind and render the plan of eternal salvation through the preceding types and shadows seen in the Old Testament. God is a God of systems. For much of my life, I had wished that I could bypass systems and processes to get to the end result of a thing. Within this process, I would have a myriad of emotions that would range from joy to pure defeat, but once the process was ended, and only if I stayed the course, I found that my making, my shaping and my faith were made in the process. Life is about process. Death is about process and all the stuff in between is process.

I think of the story of Lazarus.[9] Jesus is warned before Lazarus dies that he is sick. Lazarus is a friend of Jesus, but Jesus was not moved by urgency, He was moved by the voice of God and stuck to the plan or process. Jesus could have gone immediately, but instead He decided to wait. His waiting was a point of confusion for the disciples and his friends. He waited knowing that something greater was working and, in this beautifully-ordered chaos, life would spring again. When Jesus arrives, Lazarus is dead—dead. Lazarus was so dead that his very corpse was stinking. To say the least the situation stunk, but Jesus stayed the course. Jesus understood that there was a Holy process taking place to reveal God's power and, for that to happen, the process of death and delay had to occur.

---

[8] Genesis 5:32; 7:11, 2 Peter (NASB)
[9] John 11:1-45 (NASB)

Jesus even declared that this delay was for the Glory of God and not unto death. Imagine the dismay of those all around, even His disciples: How could life come from a dead being, but Jesus was all about bringing dead things to life.

He is still doing this to this day. What situations in your life are dead? What are you reaching for that you are praying and saying to God, "If only you had come through, the result would have been different." I want to challenge you today, and every day of your life, maybe God didn't want a different result in the moment you desired it because He was looking to perfect your process and not just give you your desired outcome. Maybe, as Job hinted, God was looking for gold "...*when I come out, there will be gold.*"[10] As we know, the end of the story is not just a resurrected Lazarus, but a whole and fully alive Lazarus! Lazarus came out of the process of death, unbounded and delivered from the very thing that seemingly destroyed him. What are you praying for? Maybe your deliverance is tied to your process and maybe your process will birth your deliverance. So instead of dreading the process, maybe embrace it. It could be the very thing you have been waiting for!

Prayer

Dear Lord,

Did anyone ever tell You that the processes You have us go through suck? Well, if not, here I am. I would

---

[10] Job 23:10 (NASB)

much rather prefer the ease of life without the process of time. Better yet, can we do away with systems that require processes that implement order? No? Okay. Now that I got that off my chest, I can cry out to You for help. All throughout Your word, I see the pattern that sometimes things must die to be resurrected or that there is a trial period that happens for people and the call on individuals' lives to be proven. I also see that that is no different with me. I know that You are taking me through a "process" for me to reach my expected end. I know that I must go through some trials to make me stronger for what You have. I also know it does not always feel good, but at this moment, I am choosing to trust and lean on You and Your process. I am choosing to lean into You, know that you are always present, always good and always with me and, if You are always with me, then even in my darkest moments I cannot be overcome. I will not be overcome. I understand that even in the moment when Lazarus himself was dead and bound, Jesus spoke life and, in a moment, he was released from the oppression that bound him. I believe that in this season You are preparing for my great release. You are awakening the things that seem dead. The things that held me bound, You are bringing me into great healing and deliverance. I know what it may look like to others and even to me in times of doubt, but today I choose to see the light and life at the end of this tunnel. You have created a process for my growth, expansion, development and abundant life, and though it's hard, I choose the process. I declare abundant life is mine, growth is mine and expansion is mine.

Finally, God, I speak to the dead things regarding marriage and relationships in my life and I say no more death! Jesus is coming to the tomb of things that I buried and that the enemy told me were dead and He is speaking life. I join with Jesus and declare life over my relationships, life over my future marriage, life over my future husband right now. I decree I am receiving all that God has and I am blooming from what looked like death, but was really a set-up from God for new life. I declare this shift now.

In Jesus' Name, Amen!

DAY 5
EMOTIONAL MATURITY

Psalm 51:10: "Create in me a clean heart, God, And renew a steadfast spirit within me."

Many people speak about maturity as if they have arrived. The older I get the more I realize that maturity is less about your natural age but more about a person's growth through time, circumstance, hardships and triumph. Maturity, no matter what the media says, is not easy to come by nor is it knowledge. Just because you have acquired knowledge and skill does not mean you have acquired maturity. When something reaches its maturation it means, in a loose sense, that it has become master in that area in regards to a situation or circumstance. When a child becomes an adult, we say that they have left puberty and reached a level of biological and biochemical maturation or maturity. Their body has stopped growing in height, their feet have stopped growing in length and, by the time they are out of puberty, there are quite a few mental developmental processes that are in the last stage of completion--that person is mature. This is why at age 18 and age 21, it is deemed that a person should be fully capable of making mature life decisions in many areas of their lives. Now, of course, we must factor in stunted growth due to deficiencies in the Five Social Determinants of Health (Economics, Health, Social Environment, Neighborhood and Education)[11] and in the Dimensions of Wellness (physical, intellectual, emotional, social, spiritual, vocational, financial, and environmental)[12] but, that aside, maturation is a natural process. However, what happens when a person is unaware of their own emotional maturity? Taking the same logic and applying it here, we understand that just because a person has knowledge and skill it does not mean that their emotional health has matured to the level of the knowledge and skill. Additionally, just because a person is advancing in age, it does not mean that their emotions are advancing at the same level. In fact, in my experience, quite the opposite is true. I have found, myself included, many people have emotional immaturity and stunted growth in our emotions. Many of us are not able to control our minds, our wills, and our emotional responses to things. For example, this is why you can have a Ph.D. professor speak in a degrading manner to a student and or cross physical boundaries with a student because their age is advanced, their knowledge advanced, but their emotions are rudimentary at best. In His Word,

---

[11] Healthy People 2030, U.S. Department of Health and Human Services, Office of Disease Prevention and Health Promotion. Retrieved [date graphic was accessed], from https://health.gov/healthypeople/objectives-and-data/social-determinants-health

[12] Stoewen DL. Dimensions of wellness: Change your habits, change your life. Can Vet J. 2017 Aug;58(8):861-862. PMID: 28761196; PMCID: PMC5508938.

God lets us know that we are to cultivate the Fruit of the Spirit[13] so that the works of the flesh which are often triggered by emotional brokenness will not rule. Not only that, but Paul tells us to "let your gentleness be known to all men,"[14] "to be angry and sin not"[15] and to "not do things out of fear, jealousy and lust."[16] There is much that the Word says in regards to our emotions, but we tend to overlook them for the gifts. The very thing the Ephesian church was rebuked for "Let there not be any bitterness, anger and wrath among you."[17] He then goes on to let them know there is another way...LOVE.

Emotional maturity is about love and letting love rule in your hearts. God is love and we are His image on the earth. If we are going to walk in Him and He in us and exemplify Him to those around us, we must challenge ourselves to grow up emotionally.

Prayer

Dear Lord,

We, the Church, often talk about spiritual maturity, but rarely do we hear an emphasis on emotional maturity. Through Your word, I know that I am required to cultivate the fruit of the spirit so that I do not give into the works of the flesh. As I cultivate this fruit, I understand that my emotions are intricately connected to this fruit or lack thereof. I also understand that,

---

[13] Gal fruit of the Spirit
[14] Let your gentleness be known to all men
[15] be angry and sin not
[16] motives
[17] Ephesians 4:31 (NASB)

as broken or as whole as they are, my emotions are my responsibility. I want to steward my heart and my life in a correct manner that is pleasing to You, but also that serves my fellow man especially those in the Body of Christ. Jesus, I understand that You came to heal me spirit, soul and body. My soul is the place where my emotions live and I know that I must be able to be aware of my emotional maturity to be able to handle the pressures of life. I realize that I have not always been aware and as a result, I have not always responded correctly or in a manner that was wise. I ask Your forgiveness for the people I have hurt and the situations that were negatively impacted due to my emotional immaturity at the time. Please cover and heal all those who were negatively affected by my emotions and my lack of maturity. Please give me eyes to see my shortcomings and the areas of my life that can grow in maturity especially when my emotions are at play. Give me ears to hear Your heart and the heart of others so that my stewardship of those people and things you have put in my hands does not suffer the consequences of my lack of maturity. I lean into You. I lean into seeing my shortcomings, knowing that, if I humble myself, You will release grace for me to be healed in my emotions and then also steward them in my interactions with people and situations. I believe that You have come to heal all of me and I receive that healing now, in Jesus' Name, Amen!

DAY 6
PASSION TO WAIT
VERSUS
POSITIONED TO WAIT

Luke 10:38-42: "Now as they were traveling along, He entered a village; and a woman named Martha welcomed Him into her home. And she had a sister called Mary, who was also seated at the Lord's feet, and was listening to His word. But Martha was distracted with all her preparations; and she came up to Him and said, 'Lord, do You not care that my sister has left me to do the serving by myself? Then tell her to help me.' But the Lord answered and said to her, 'Martha, Martha, you are worried and distracted by many things; but only one thing is necessary; for Mary has chosen the good part, which shall not be taken away from her.'"

Mary and Martha exemplify passion v position. Both loved their dear friend and Rabbi more than life itself. They loved Him so much that they could not wait for Him to come to their house and dine. Imagine, the King of Glory coming to your house. Well, this is exactly what was taking place. Jesus was showing up to their house to share His heart with His disciples. What an honor! If Jesus was coming to their house, it was purposeful, intentional and strategic. I believe that both Mary and Martha knew this and neither took it lightly. I can imagine the night before both barely able to sleep with whispers in their hearts regarding His arrival. Mary thinking, "Oh my, I can't want to hear His words and sit and study what He has to say" and Martha thinking, "I can't wait to get up and start preparation for His time here. Everything must be perfect." Both women were in anticipation for Jesus' arrival. Perhaps, both lie awake imagining what it would look and be like. Perhaps, both knew the perfect strategy to maximize their time with Jesus for His powerful arrival. However, in this story, we see that there was a greater emphasis on what was better or most expedient in the eyes of Jesus. The thing that was most expedient was the very thing rooted in one's position and not just passion. There was a fervent outward passion that Martha exhibited. Her preparation was undeniable and no doubt flawless, but there was something missing: the position/motive of her heart. Jesus tells Martha that she is simply too anxious about too many things and that Mary choosing to sit and be still was the better part.

Martha had passion and Mary had position. How often in our lives are we hurried and doing things out of passion or a fervent desire to be productive, but haven't stopped to consider are we in the right position? How many times are we passionate even about good things like fasting, prayer, preaching and winning souls, but we haven't positioned ourselves to know the will of God, for our lives, in this very thing? I believe Mary was thinking, "It is not often that Jesus shows up, and when He does, I want to make sure I hear Him." How many of us are in a hurry trying to become the perfect mate or do all the things to be appealing to our future spouse, but none of us are actually still before the King knowing that is the thing that actually positions us for stewarding our season well and receiving all that God has for us? I remember many years ago when I first received the vision for Whole Single Woman, the Lord said "many women don't know what their purpose is for their lives because they are not doing 1 Corinthians 7:34. They are not abiding in me and focused on me for what I have for them." As a single woman, our primary goal is to press into Jesus and from that other things will flow. I once said this statement and it still rings true "Maybe you are still single, so you can learn how to pray." To adapt it here, I say this to you "Maybe you are still single, to learn His voice, to sit at His feet and choose the better part." Passion is a beautiful thing, but passion without awareness of your current season/position can have you focused on so many things, and many good things, but not always the better things.

When I met Kenny, I was focused on God and I had learned the art of praying for my mate while actively waiting on my Beloved, Jesus. It can be a challenging balance, but oh the joy of knowing that sitting at His feet is the correct posture and place God wants to give you your desires. I spent many days resting at His feet so that when Kenny came I could hear "This is my beloved son in whom I am well pleased." I could hear God's heart for me regarding him.

Prayer

Dear Lord,

I don't just want to have passion about this life or be passionate in this life, but I want to correctly discern the hour of Your visitation that I may hear and know You and Your will. Martha was an amazing woman and I desire and ask for her diligence, but I ask that the root of my productivity and activity is not an anxious heart, but that the root is simply a heart to hear and know You--a heart longing for love for her Savior. This type of love produces a God-like faith and faith, even if it is small, can move mountains. As I wait and prepare, let not my time only be spent on exhorting energy on things that feel so big, but let my time be spent on the things that please Your heart and draw me closer to You. I confess my time with You has been lacking and therefore, Your voice feels distant and strained in my life. I am returning now to You. I am returning to Your word. As much as I want the promise of a mate and all that You have for me in this life, I want You and Your voice even more. Give me the grace of Mary to sit at Your feet to be positioned for the promise and joy in the waiting. Let me be motivated by intimacy with You and let me only be moved by Your presence. I declare that nothing will hinder the receiving of Your promise. I decree that I am positioned in the wait and faith is fueled by love for You.

I declare that I will not miss the season and time of Your visitation, but I will be positioned to hear Your voice and from that place my passion arises. I am in sync with You at Your feet and because of this, I have not only chosen the better part, I am receiving God's best for me.

In Jesus' Name, Amen!

DAY 7
REDEMPTION FROM
THE PAST

John 21:15-17: "Now when they had finished breakfast, Jesus* said to Simon Peter, 'Simon, son of John, do you love Me more than these?' He said to Him*, 'Yes, Lord; You know that I love You.' He* said to him, 'Tend My lambs.' He* said to him again, a second time, 'Simon, son of John, do you love Me?' He said to Him*, 'Yes, Lord; You know that I love You.' He* said to him, 'Shepherd My sheep.' He* said to him the third time, 'Simon, son of John, do you love Me?' Peter was hurt because He* said to him the third time, 'Do you love Me?' And he said to Him*, 'Lord, You know all things; You know that I love You.' Jesus* said to him, 'Tend My sheep.'"

*E*ver been in denial? Well, if not, read the story of Peter found in Luke 22. During Christ's betrayal and subsequent court trial, Peter is questioned three times by individuals who had proof that Peter was an associate and disciple of Christ. Peter was in the same vicinity of the trial of Christ. While in proximity of his Savior and Friend, he was faced with the greatest challenge of his life.

"Do I confess Christ or Deny Him?" Well, spoiler alert: Peter denies Christ just as Jesus had predicted. The cock crows and Peter's betrayal is set. Imagine being Peter, denying the One you loved after He saved you from your former life, changed your name and spoke destiny over you. How do you think Peter felt? The One Man who saved Peter and his family from starvation and debt and now, he could not even acknowledge Him. I imagine Peter felt regret, shame and condemnation. I imagine he was in pain. Well, in John 21, Jesus provides a healing balm to the days of agony Peter was wallowing in--Jesus healed him. In John 21, Jesus rebutted every denial by allowing Peter to confess his weak yet sincere love for Jesus. Three times Jesus asks Peter, "Do you love me?" and Peter verbally declares his love for Jesus three times. It is at this moment that Jesus responds with a directive that spoke to the calling on Peter's life: since you love me, "Feed my sheep."[18] It was like Jesus was washing away the denial and reminding Peter of what He was called to--He was reminding Peter that He was greater than his past. In a sense, I believe, Jesus wanted to remind him that his love, though imperfect, was still enough to be used by Him.

Jesus comes not just to help us identify our missteps, wrongs and shortcomings, but Jesus comes to say, "Despite your shortcomings, I still have a plan and if you come to me no matter how weak your confession, I will meet you there." How often do we not go to God because of shame of the past? How often do we linger in the agony that comes from us falling short? There is no receiving of redemption without confession.[19] We must come to

---

[18] John 21:17 (NASB)
[19] Romans 10:10 (NASB)

Him with all our weakness and our faults, and when He calls out to us, we must respond with a choice to love Him again and again. God will not only meet you in that love, but He will release grace to love Him more. I have ministered to many women who don't even feel worthy of love after they fall short, but God has more. He wants humanity to know that the imperfection was calculated into the salvation equation.[20] Therefore, if Peter can be redeemed from denying Jesus during the time when he actually walked with Him, how much more is redemption extended to us who simply believe because of the disciples' word?[21] God wants to redeem your past and remind you of the destiny He has called you to.

Prayer

Dear Jesus,

Who is a God like You that can take the past and bring full redemption? No one. It is very easy to live in the past. The skeletons of addiction, perversion and iniquity sometimes feel very much attached to me. It sometimes feels like I cannot get away from the dead man that You saved me from. Sometimes newness in You feels so far. However, it is in these moments where the past feels so real that I choose to hear Your voice calling me higher and further into destiny. I choose to release myself again and again from the chains of the past and I choose to

---

[20] Romans 5:8, 1 John 2:1-2 (NASB)
[21] John 20:29 (NASB)

boldly walk in the identity that You pronounce over me. Your Word is Truth and I know that freeing me from the past is what You specialize in. Freedom is why You came. So, Lord, I ask that You would renew my mind and help me to see my life as You see my life. Help me to see my circumstance as You see my circumstance. Help me to embrace the truth of being a new creation in Christ. I choose to believe that no matter what I have done and no matter who I was in the past, I am new and ready and redeemed in You.

I identify the lies that I battle with daily (list your lies here):

1. Lie: I will always be addicted to sexual perversion (example)

2.

3.

4.

5.

6.

7.

8.

9.

10.

I choose to believe the truth of God's word that says (write what God says):

1. Truth: I am free in God and whom the Son sets free is free indeed.[22] (example)

2.

3.

4.

5.

6.

7.

8.

9.

10.

---

[22] John 8:36 (NASB)

On the basis of these declarations that are founded on Your Word, I believe that You have redeemed me and my past and that I am no longer the same. I am a new creation and I am not bound by sin, but I am more than an overcomer (Romans 8:31-39).

In Jesus' Name, Amen!

DAY 8
POTENTIAL IN THE PRESENT

Jeremiah 29:11: "'For I know the plans that I have for you,' declares the LORD, 'plans for prosperity and not for disaster, to give you a future and a hope.'"

The ability to have a vision for the future is a beautiful gift, especially when there are little-to-no signs of fruitfulness in your present. Israel was in this place. In Jeremiah 29, there is a recap of their current state of captivity. God speaks to them where they are and, while in exile, He reminds them the best way to remember the promises for their life is to gain hope and be fruitful where they are and they would see what He has. So, while in captivity, God commands them to be fruitful in every way while there. He says "Build houses and live in them; and plant gardens and eat their produce. Take wives and father sons and daughters, and take wives for your sons and give your daughters to husbands, so that they may give birth to sons and daughters; and grow in numbers there and do not decrease. Seek the prosperity of the city where I have sent you into exile, and pray to the LORD on its behalf; for in its prosperity will be your prosperity."[23] And, then the famous verse (v11): "For I know what I've planned for you." Often, we skip over verses 1-10 to get to verse 11, but verses 1-10 are so important to understanding verse 11. God basically said, I know where you are and things don't look good. You are in bondage and exile to Babylon, a pagan nation and you are discouraged, but I need you to strengthen yourselves spiritually, mentally, emotionally, physical and materially because of where I am taking you. God's command here was not to wait until the promise of deliverance arrived (it was still a ways off), but the command was because of what I have for you in the future, it is important that you prepare yourselves now. I can imagine the Israelites were astonished. Many of them were listening to false prophets not speaking the Word of God and it was causing confusion. But, God spoke very clearly *"...now is the time right where you are to increase yourself..."* Don't sit on your hands and wait for the future promise, but see My goodness right where you are—this manifests a vision for the future. For vision to manifest, it must be clear and it must be actionable. Today you must decide that no matter where you are or what you are doing you will have a clear vision, it will be actionable and that you will take steps in the present towards it. You must hear the word of the Lord. How many single ladies have I come across who have said: "When I get married, I will travel. When I get married, I will do ministry. Or, when I get married, I will write that book because at that point my husband will be caring for everything and can just do

---

[23] Jeremiah 29:5-7 (NASB)

the things in my heart." This is a false narrative you are creating for your life. You must ask God, "What is it that I must put my hands to right here and now that will help to manifest the promises for the future season?" If you ask, He will answer. Your job is to put your life in God's hands and allow Him to direct you in each season as to what you should do. I am so glad I had the experiences I did before marriage. It made me enjoy my husband and what God was calling us to that much more because I had NO REGRETS. Like Israel in Jeremiah 29, you want to have no regrets. You want to sow and reap right where you are because this is just a small taste of the harvest to come. God wants you to experience His good things even while you wait on the fullness, so trust your season, trust the process and ask God for clear actionable vision, so you have NO REGRETS!

Prayer

Dear Abba,

Sometimes my present circumstances can feel so overwhelming and can make me feel as though I am drowning in the day-to-day that I find it hard to look into the future. So often I am guilty of drowning in the present, in seeing what You have not done, that I cannot see what is happening right in front of me or what You are saying. Additionally, sometimes I get so focused on where I am that I can't even begin to believe in Your goodness for now or for what is to come. I understand that my ability to have a vision for the future is directly connected to my ability to hear and see You in the present. I understand that my future is connected to my present. Forgive me for all the times that I could not see where I was or how You were moving in my present. Forgive me for being so focused on what wasn't that I could not see the potential blessing in what is. Help me to turn my attention to You and Your voice in every season. Just as You told the Children of Israel to be fruitful in a place of captivity, I choose to believe that in the seasons leading up to the promises You have for me, that there is fruit to be harvested and blessing to be had. I decree and declare that as I walk in my present moments with intentionality, clarity and faith, that my breakthrough is assured and on the way. I decree and declare that my future is better as I hope in the present for the promises of God. I choose to take my eyes off of what isn't and choose to see the potential in what is. In my job, I choose to bless You right where I am. In my relationship status, I choose to bless You for right where I am. In my family, I choose to bless You for right where I am. I choose at every moment to praise my way into the breakthrough, for I know that as I do this, You are renewing my strength and the plans You have for me are "yes" and "amen." I declare "yes" and "amen" over my life today as I prepare for the greater right where I am.

In Jesus' Name, Amen!

DAY 9
A NEW THING

Isaiah 43:18-19: *"Do not call to mind the former things, Or consider things of the past. Behold, I am going to do something new. Now it will spring up; Will you not be aware of it? I will even make a roadway in the wilderness, Rivers in the desert."*

I love shiny new things. Ask Kenny! A lot of jewelry I have at home is made up of lots of bling; so much so, I can't wear it every day because it is too dramatic for the Vans and chucks I so love to wear! Anyway, the truth remains I like new things. As much as this is true, I don't always like when new things happen. In a 2019 Forbes article, the author identified that "grief is part of change."[24] I once heard it described this way "All people consider all change as loss."[25] As beautiful as new things are and as beautiful as the result of new things may be, when anything requires change

---

[24] Brian Gorman, "The Grief of Change," Forbes. July 3, 2019, https://www.forbes.com/sites/forbescoachescouncil/2019/07/03/the-grief-of-change/?sh=1977c73350e2

[25] unknown

there is a process of loss that must accompany it. I've watched the dramatically amazing things that have happened in my life and I can remember that in the midst of all the celebration of the new thing there was a little feeling in the pit of my emotions made up of grief. Grieving the old and praising the new. When something new has happened, it does not mean that the old was bad, but it does mean that it is time for a change. I am reminded of the children of Israel. In their case, they needed a change. They were in captivity in Babylon and they needed a word that something would change. God was using their captivity to grow, develop and prepare them for the future promise. And so, in the midst of their misfortune, God delivers a reminder that their present was not their promise, but that now is the time for a new thing to happen.

In this reminder, He tells them to leave the past in the past and to not hold on to it, because He wanted to do something totally new! He shows the lengths He would take to manifest what they saw as impossible: a roadway in the wilderness and rivers in the desert. I find it very clever of God to refer to their wandering in the wilderness and desert after their freedom from Egypt. God was saying I am going to do something so new that it will remind you of the mighty deliverance I brought many years ago: It will be nothing short of miraculous.

God's reminder of what He wanted to do while pulling on imagery of what He had already done, was to awaken their hearts with faith for the God of the impossible. Many of us need a "new thing" to happen in our lives. Whether it is a job, a house, friends or a mate, the impossible is staring down at us. But, today, God wants to awaken our hearts to a new thing. What is it that you don't have faith for, but you feel is God's will? Could it be that God wants to miraculously do a new thing? I know the new can seem scary especially when the old is so normal, but remember if God is wanting to bring you into a new place or allow you to have new experiences, it is time to trust Him. It is so very important to learn the depths of your faith prior to marriage and to believe God for the impossible prior to a mate.

Maybe you are in the place of the impossible so God can do a new thing. Maybe God is challenging you to move to a new city or take a new job or join a new church so He can do the new thing. I will never forget saying, "I will never find my husband in Pittsburgh!" It was in that place that he found me and it was my connection to that city that linked us together. It, in fact, was a new thing! At the time, I did not see finding my mate while living there to be possible. Boy, was I wrong! I challenge you today to take the limits off, open yourself up to possibility and embrace the new thing!

Prayer

Dear Lord,

I set my eyes on You and not on what is around me. I look to Jesus the Author and the Perfecter of my faith. Give me eyes to see the way You do. Give me a heart to understand the way You do. You see people, places and things so differently than I do. Where I see desolation and despair, you see fruitfulness and abundance. Where

I see regret and disappointment,
You see beauty and wisdom. You are able to take ashes
and make beauty. You are able to give joy for mourning.
You are able to give praise for heaviness and this reality
helps me to see that You are able to do a new thing.
Father, it is You and Your abilities that I align with. Even
when it is uncomfortable and my trust is weak, I will
call out to you to do the new thing you want to do. Lord,
show me now the areas of my life that you are wanting
to shift and change. I partner with you to allow myself
to be challenged for the new. I know you have been
pressing me to change _____
(list something you feel He is challenging you in) and today
I say yes. I know that your full promise may not be
where I am now so I open myself up to the stretching
and I believe You will give me the capacity to say yes to
the new and unfamiliar. I am Yours. I align my heart
with Your will and I say "yes" to Your heart for me in
this season and every season thereafter. You know the
plans You have for me.

In Jesus' Name, Amen!

DAY 10
NO FEAR.
NO ANXIETY.

2 Tim 1:7: "For God has not given us a spirit of timidity, but of power and love and discipline."

I cannot tell you the amount of times I did not do something simply because of fear. I also cannot tell you the amount of times that I have allowed fear to impact the quality of my life. For both, the times have been countless. As strong and "fearless" as I like to believe I am, I have lacked confidence in many areas of my life. This lack of confidence has led to self-doubt and disbelief. As a result, there have been countless times where I have not stepped out in faith. Why was this? Because of fear. Fear can take on many different forms. Anger can be expressed as fear. Timidity can show as fear. Shame and control are in the immediate family of fear. These are just a few forms that fear takes on.

How I saw fear in my own life was often fear of rejection/ abandonment, fear of man and fear of failure. These three manifestations of fear held me in bondage for large portions of my life. When I was young, I had an experience where I was imprinted with abandonment and rejection. I felt that, in this situation, no one came to my rescue and, because of it, I feared that others would leave me or not be there for me. It was heavily rooted in my subconscious mind and, when in relationship with others, I would never have peace. There was a gnawing sense in my stomach that people would leave me and not be able to rescue me. Due to the understandable frailty and imperfection of man, this fear was reinforced many times when others failed me. This fear would isolate and leave me feeling alone.

Another fear was the fear of man. And boy oh boy, did this one have a grip on me. Fear of man and fear of failure would often appear as twins in my subconscious. There was no denying they were both there. Because of my personality type and my experiences, I often felt like I had to be the person who had to have it all together. When your world spins out of control and you grow up fast, you learn how to control the fragmented pieces of your life to make sure you are able to still grow and progress. Because of this, I developed a perfectionist mindset and I never wanted to do anything wrong. If I failed, I had an ungodly belief that my failure would cause the world to spin out of control and that that spinning would be attributed to my failure. Thus, man would see me as a failure and I not only would be letting myself but ALL others down. This ungodly belief caused me to fear what man thought of me in my failure. I was constantly worried about what leaders, relatives, and friends thought of me. Some even wanted me to feel this responsibility to minimize their own. However, at some point, I had to let it go. In the spring of 2020, I almost broke under the weight of responsibility. It was in that moment with voices swirling around in my head that I heard God say, "I get to tell you who you are!" His booming voice sat King on my mind and stood as the authority over my identity. At that moment, the fear of man broke off of me. I was not ruled by the opinions of others, but by the One who called me to begin with. Why do I share this? Because fear is controlling and debilitating. It hinders and stops one's true self from coming forth. It was in this moment with God, that I released my fear, said "no" to anxiety and chose to rest in His promise and His identity for me. Your challenge today is to release fear and choose peace, rest and your true identity in God.

Prayer

Dear Lord,

I am all too aware of fear. I often let it cripple me in many ways, including _____,

_____, _____,

_____. I now see that this is not okay.
Allowing fear to handicap me gives in to the enemy's plans for my life and keeps me from walking in the full potential of the plans that You have for my life. I repent. I repent for walking in fear. I repent for even holding fear as my friend and using it as a defense mechanism to protect me from situations and circumstances. Fear is not of God. I know that Your Word lets me know that even my best effort bathed in fear is sin (Romans 14:22-

23). I do not want to live a life with the works or fruit of fear, but I want to live a life with the works and fruit of confidence and boldness and of knowing who I am in You. Today, Father, is my day to take my present and future back by walking in boldness. Today is the day that You redeem my past by healing me of fear. I will not give in. I choose today to be my day of freedom. I will not fear my future or allow fear to creep into my prayer life or my desires. What You have for me is good and this is my confession. I declare: "No more fear!"

In Jesus' Name, Amen!

DAY 11
FIND PURPOSE

————◆———————◆————

*James 1:2-4: "Consider it all joy, my brothers and sisters, when you encounter various trials, knowing that the testing of your faith produces endurance. And let endurance have its perfect result, **so that you may be perfect and complete, lacking in nothing.**"*

Perseverance is not easy. It requires endurance and focus in order to achieve a specific outcome. It requires going through. However, going through is not all bad. James let us know that the end result of perseverance is being "perfect, entire and lacking nothing."[26] I remember when God gave this to me. I was sitting in a prayer room in Kansas City, bemoaning about my singleness and I could hear Him so clearly "...that you may be perfect and entire, lacking nothing." I knew He was saying, "I want you lacking nothing, Adrianna." This was not to say I would not need my husband when he came or that I would even achieve every life goal by the time he

---

[26] James 1:4 (NKJV)

came, but what it did mean was that I was no longer going to be looking on the outside for what can only be satisfied from Christ on the inside. It was time for me to stop looking on the outside. It was time for me to prepare my heart for the spiritual and natural blessings that God had in store. How did I do that? Intimacy with Him. When we are laser focused on Him, we find our purpose and our destiny and, when we find that, we can pursue accomplishing His will by stewarding God-assignments. Let today be the day that you choose to say "yes" to perseverance and "yes" to finding purpose in Him.

Prayer

Dear Lord,

So often I give up. So often I am willing to let go. The place of waiting is so challenging and difficult. I feel the pain of the wait daily and though I know that I want to wait on You and I want to be productive where I am, so often I am overwhelmed by the reality that I am still waiting. I confess that this makes me want to give up and just stop everything. I confess it makes me have feelings of anger towards You and others. And, I confess that it makes me fall into comparison. I also confess that You are the only one who can give me strength and understanding in this place. Even when You feel distant and far away, I choose to confess that You are close and near to me and that You see me. I choose to confess that You have commissioned this place of the wait. In

James 1, You give me the blueprint on how to deal with the trials and testing seasons of my life. You tell me to consider it joy. I understand that You do not tell me to simply feel joy, but you tell me to consider it a joyous thing when trials and testing come my way because there is something bigger working in me. I know there is something bigger working in me. My faith being tried is working in me a greater measure of glory that will be revealed--I declare that. According to Your word, this faith produces perseverance. This is the ability to persevere. The ability to push through. The ability to not give up. I not only look to myself, but to all those who have gone before me. The "Faith Hall of Fame" found in Hebrews 11. Through perseverance, they received the very things they were believing in You for and so today, by grace I choose to persevere. Their perseverance gave them purpose and purpose makes us fruitful and productive. I desire to be fruitful and productive. I desire to have purpose and produce from this season. It is my honest prayer and declaration that today, I choose to hold on to what I know. I know that in this place of waiting if I persevere, I will not be shaken. I will not be moved and I will receive what You promised. Today, I choose your promises. I choose faith in the wait and even now You are giving me strength.

In Jesus' Name, Amen!

DAY 12
VISION AND ITS
APPLICATION

Proverbs 29:18: "Where there is no vision, the people are unrestrained, But happy is one who keeps the Law."

I can't tell you how important vision is. Proverbs tells us that without it people perish or cast off appropriate boundaries and restraints for their lives. They live outside of what is appropriate for them. When I was a young girl, I had lots of vision and there were many things I wanted to do, but in the midst of the vision, I needed eyes to see. Habakkuk 2:2-3 reminds us to write the vision and make it plain that those who read it or who have eyes to see it may run with it. It is not just seeing and reading the vision, it is the ability to discern the vision within the season of the manifestation of the vision. In my teens, 20s and a few years into my 30s, I often made a very similar mistake. I had a vision for my life and sometimes when something looked like the vision, I would go hard after that thing only to be disappointed. As a result, I had a lot of trial-and-error on how to work the vision of my life. In my mid 30s, I realized that in some areas I was not seeing correctly. I had the vision and I saw it, but only for what I understood it to be and not in its fullness. I heard the word and I wrote the word, but discerning the Word requires spiritual foresight and aptitude. I felt like in my teens and 20s, I was constantly getting a crash course in seeing things rightly. I was also being challenged on how to handle the Word of the Lord correctly. So, after much prayer, I learned a new prayer: "Give me new eyes." This type of prayer allows God to reform and reprogram any unknowing glitches in your spiritual operating system aka your spiritual vision that can cause you to mishandle and misinterpret your vision. Does this mean your vision will change? Not necessarily. But, it does mean that your vision can be tweaked, upgraded and even expanded to fully see its role and capacity in your life. You have to be willing to understand the vision and its place during the varied seasons of your life. Asking God for "eyes to see" will help your spiritual senses to be awakened and focus in on the application of the vision of your life.

So, I encourage you to not just get a vision for your life, but give you eyes to run with the correct interpretation of your vision along with the correct vantage point from which to view it one season at a time.

Eyes to see.

Prayer

Lord,

I need new eyes. I know that You spoke and released

an amazing vision into my life before I was born and then You expounded upon it year after year, but to be honest sometimes I feel lost in regards to it. Sometimes I feel like I am not seeing it correctly or I wonder maybe I interpreted it incorrectly. Often, I feel like I can't see it at all. I now know that it is not enough to just have vision, but to have eyes to see that vision in every season of my life and to correctly interpret that vision in every season. I don't just want to see, but I want to see rightly. I remember the ways that I have gotten ahead of You in the past because I thought I was walking out the vision of my life correctly, only to find out I was in error. I don't want to wander in darkness again. I don't want to run with a vision out of season and out of time. I want to be able to have a plan for my vision. Some things I will accomplish in my 20s and other things in my 30s and still other things in my 40s and 50s. To everything there is a season and I want to have eyes to see the season and the application of vision by wisdom. So today I commit to walking with You day by day and moment by moment. I commit to not get ahead of You and by your grace to walk hand in hand with You as you reveal the beauty story You have for me. I know that my ability to be connected to you, is directly connected to my receiving of the promises You have for me. I commit myself to having eyes to see.

In Jesus' Name, Amen!

DAY 13
DIVINE CONNECTIONS

Proverbs 27:17: *"As iron sharpens iron, So one person sharpens another."*

One of the biggest blessings in my life have been divine connections, relationships, and friendships. In fact, I would dare say that they have saved my life many a day. It has been because of divine connections that I am where I am today. It has also been because of them that I am not somewhere else. I can remember a simple prayer that I prayed when I was entering into my senior year of high school, "Lord, please don't let me go through my senior year without any friends." You see, prior to this, and during my 11th grade year, I had lost some pretty close friends. I want to say that I don't know what happened, but I do. It was God. God saw the path that I was traveling down and He knew I had no business being on that path, so He rerouted me. I fit into a few different circles, but there was a group of female friends that were closest to me. We did everything together including sleepovers. I knew the drama in their families and they knew the drama of mine, but that type of intimacy was not enough. God wanted me to have a divine cry for more--for relationships that were headed toward destiny and not just focused on temporal satisfaction. I want to say, those women are great! They are amazing women who are moving and shaking within their spheres of influence, but I felt a pull towards a different path for my life and for my destiny and it needed to begin when I was 16 years old. God needed to reroute me for the call that was on my life. He wanted me to plunge into the depths of who He was and, to get me to focus on that, all of my comfort zones needed to be challenged and removed. When they were, I cried out to God to provide and satisfy me with relationships that were headed into my future that were either blessed or orchestrated by Him. I say blessed or orchestrated because not every relationship and the fullness of it was exactly God's picture of perfection, but He did use them all to make me into the person I would become in my 20's and 30's: His Glory and my good.

I have watched the hand of God curate season after season of my life. I learned some valuable lessons and some hard ones too. I learned how to steward friendships and how to forgive. I learned how to hold on too long and the importance of letting go. I learned how to be an echo of others and how to be a voice for God. Finally, I learned how God will connect you divinely with others to remind you of who you are. All of these things I learned through divine connections. Relationships are important to God. Each one in your life has its place and it is your job to pray about each one and see what their purpose is in your life. All the relationships, whether orchestrated or blessed, were used for my good.

Whether it was when I worked at the United Nations with my college mentor or received dramatic and timely healing from Restoring the Foundations Deliverance ministers, God's hand was on it all, bringing me into covenant for a time, a season or a lifetime. It was His hand that showed me the importance of divine connections. This day, I can proudly say that the friendships that I have now are God ordered and most praised!

Prayer

Dear Lord,

I haven't always valued connectivity in my life. Sometimes, I even despised it. Due to fear or shame, I kept peers, mentors and mentees away. I don't want to do that again. I want to accept every person You have in my life, knowing they will help me get to the next place You have for my life. Forgive me for not valuing relationships as You do and forgive me for taking them for granted. Forgive me for being a lone ranger at times and for pushing against Your connections for me. Most importantly, forgive me for not seeing them. I know there were times You encouraged me to befriend someone or trust a leader and because my eyes and heart were not open, I could not see. Forgive me again. I want to see those connections and hear Your heart for those whom you have placed in my life. Help me to take inventory and help me to embrace the new and different. Lord, I declare today, that I want every connection that You have for my life. Divine connections lead to divine growth which lead to divine encounters. I want it all! Any space in me that is resistant to these connections, reveal it that I may repent of it and then remove it and fill it with the wisdom and character of Christ. Holy Spirit, I need You in this season and I want You in this season. Help me to recognize divine connections.

In Jesus' name, Amen!

Take a moment and write down three individuals that God is highlighting to you that you feel you may need to connect with in this next season.

DAY 14
WHOLE SINGLE WOMAN,
YOU MADE IT!

II Corinthians 5:17: "Therefore if any man be in Christ, he is a new creature: old things are passed away; behold, all things are become new."

PART I

We are on day 14. Day 14 is a glorious day. It is the day where you build on the last 13 days by releasing these handpicked decrees over yourself. Additionally, you get to craft a few of your own. My own walk with the Lord has been one marked by healing and deliverance. I was one who always spoke negatively about myself, my situation and my destiny. Laden with anger and depression, I often found it hard to speak words of life. The only problem with that is when you are created by a God of power your words and actions have power. The negative words would bear negative fruit in my life. However, I learned that the closer I got to God the Father the more he healed and delivered and the more he did that my words changed.

If you should remember one thing regarding your words, let it be that life and death respond to the words that do or do not come out of your mouth. In the past, I would give in to the nudges of shame, fear, control and depression. I would often think to myself, "I will never be anything, I will amount to nothing, I will always fear, no one will ever want me, I am stupid, I am ugly, I am a failure, I am abandoned and so many more lies. As my therapist shockingly said to me, "If you didn't share what you did, I would have never known the struggles you were having." On the outside you would not be able to see this, but these lies of the enemy were there often and often I agreed with them! It would not be until I realized that my words were giving life to my dark language and, the more that I spoke these phrases, the more I believed them. And the more I believed them, the more I partnered with Satan to speak death into my life. It is like listening to sad music while you are sad or listening to music about a broken heart when you have a broken heart. What does it do? It makes you despondent and hopeless. And that was where I was. No matter the amount of degrees, successful business ventures, and foreign ministry trips where I saw God move, nothing could change the bondage that was produced by my language. Oh, but we praise God! The moment I realized the power of my words and declared the truth of God's Word over my own life is when I saw the power of those words come to pass. Listen woman of God, God has called you to Life. And, His Words are spirit and life. Even without full belief in the phrases inspired by scripture, I began to say them--one by one. This leap of faith has made all the difference in how I navigate the world around me and the different circumstances I find myself in.

Below are just a few you can say, as well!

Declarations

"I am not rejected. I am accepted, I am wanted, I am loved, I am valuable, I am necessary."

"I am not fat and ugly. I am beautifully and wonderfully made."

"I am a daughter of the King. I am accepted and adopted by Him."

"I have the joy of the Lord."

"I walk in peace and grace."

PART II

Now that you have journeyed with the Lord for 14 days, I believe it is so important to cultivate a prayer life for your future mate. I find that many women struggle with either prayer in general or with the notion that they can't effectively contend for their mate while keeping their eyes on Jesus. But, it is possible! The two are not contrary to one another. We are supposed to pray earnestly for God's will (marriage) and also fall more in love with Jesus (intimacy).

This is a guided journal and so the following seven prompts will begin with a heading as to how you will pray for your husband. If you have taken my 21 Days With Him free webinar, you will have had step by step guidance leading you into this in a community-based atmosphere. If you have not taken it, do not worry! The prompts are clear and concise. You will follow the pattern of the last 14 days and maybe jump on my next 21 Days With Him class!

Directions:

1. Identify the heading and read through the scriptures.

2. Personally identify any additional scriptures you would like to use.

3. Journal regarding your thoughts about the heading.

4. Write out a prayer for your husband.

The purpose of the following journal entries is not perfection. It is for your weak prayers to be released to God and watch how God answers. It is His super on your natural!

If you follow these simple steps, do the 21 days repeatedly and then continue to craft your own prayers to accompany this journal, you will find that you will slowly transform into a prayer warrior for the healing of your present, the pathway of your future and for the future of your marriage. Prayer is so vital and key to our destinies and through these next seven days, I know that you will be ignited with passion to pray for your husband and inspired to join with the Great Intercessor [29] as He prepares you for what has already been prepared for you.[30]

---

[29] Romans 8:34 (NASB)

[30] Bishop Joseph Garlington. Sermon.

DAY 15
SALVATION
John 3:16; 1 Timothy 2:4

───────────

Journal

Prayer/Declarations

DAY 16
SANCTIFICATION
1 Thess 5:23; 2 Tim 2:21

Journal

Prayer/Declarations

DAY 17
RESTORATION
Matt 6:33; Gal 6:1

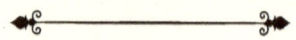

Journal

Prayer/Declarations

DAY 18
HEALING

3 John 1:2; Jeremiah 17:14

Journal

Prayer/Declarations

DAY 19
WHOLENESS
Jeremiah 30:17; Psalm 29:11

Journal

Prayer/Declarations

DAY 20
PROSPERITY

2 Corinthians 9:8, Deuteronomy 8:18

Journal

Prayer/Declarations

DAY 21
MATURITY, GROWTH
AND WISDOM

Luke 2:52; 1 Corinthians 14:20

Journal

Prayer/Declarations

THE CONCLUSION: CONTINUE ON WITH HIM

This book was simple, but I hope you found it profound. I hope you found yourself in the pages of this book and that you found yourself developing an open and honest communication with God. I hope you found growth.

As many of you know, I am very big on transparency. This has been my lifeline. I would encourage you as you move forward in growth that you find 1-3 individuals that you can be accountable to and that can be a support to you. Too often single ladies are lone rangers in their hearts and minds and the outcome is not favorable. Why sit sad and depressed when there is a woman who could lift you up and vice versa. We are meant for community and relationships. God has those specific few that are designed for you.

Lastly, the local church is a big part of our faith as believers. The 1st century church gave us a model of discipleship. My prayer for you is that during your healing you would find a solid local church with trustworthy leaders who can deliver the message of faith and truth to strengthen you in your walk.

Whether single or married, a journey with God is the route He requires for us to receive the best for us. Don't let your journey end in 21 days. Let this be part of the voyage of a lifetime!

Sincerely,
Adrianna